RON HOLLOWAY

A COURTESY FLUSH GOES A LONG WAY

10 COURTESY FLUSHES TO CLEAR THE AIR

STRATEGIES

Printed in the United States of America

www.iamronholloway.com

First Printing, 2015

ISBN-13: 978-0-692-46154-9
ISBN-10: 069246154X
Library of Congress Control Number: 2015943783

To:
my mother for her nearly impossible feat of being a woman while raising a man;
my wife and family for their unconditional love and support;
all veterans, servicemen and servicewomen for their selflessness;
Nelson Mandela simply by virtue of who he was; and
to all the people with the attention span of a goldfish.

cour·te·sy flush (ˈkərdəsē/ / fləSH/)
verb; the showing of politeness in one's attitude while de-
toxifying on the toilet by causing large quantities of water
to pass through in order to reduce foul aroma

RON HOLLOWAY

A COURTESY FLUSH GOES A LONG WAY

10 COURTESY FLUSHES TO CLEAR THE AIR

STRATEGIES

Contents

Introduction

Inside awaits a planetarium swirling with star-studded philosophical values, attitudes, and beliefs worth implementing right now in your life and sharing with others.

How do you handle stress and pressure? Do you need help managing personal relationships? Are you clueless about how to ignite real concrete change in your life? Whether you are overcoming a tough break-up or looking to make a major life change, A Courtesy Flush Goes a Long Way, gives you a fresh guide to feeling healthier, less stressed and more clear-minded.

Struggling with the "ups and downs" of life as we all do, I wrote this book to share the spirituality, actions and philosophical strategies that saved my life, which will help shape and redefine yours. Each flush gives concise, "hard-hitting" advice, answers, one-liner tips, and stories to help you reach the best person you can be. So, if you want some "smell good" and clean air, get ready. Follow along. Listen more. There's a toilet with your name on it.

Flush

①

Don't settle
for mud butt:
Get out of your
own way

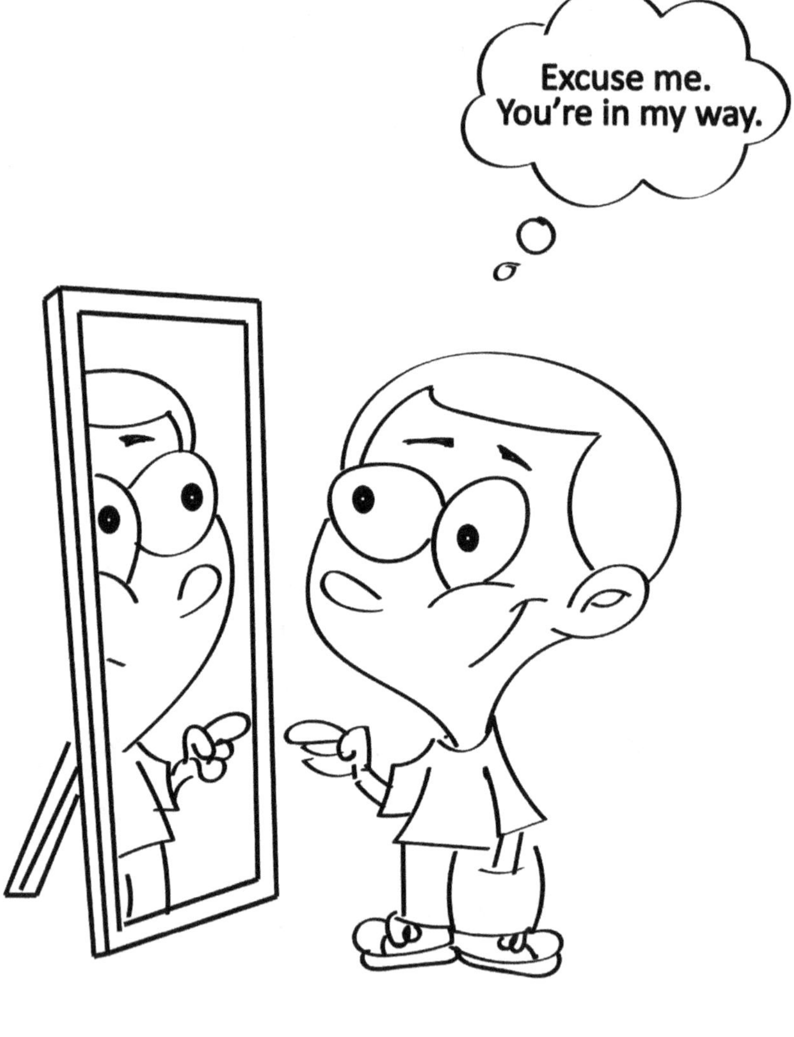
Excuse me.
You're in my way.

Do you remember Pig-Pen from Charlie Brown? I loved him although I'm almost certain he had "mud butt." In a nutshell, "mud butt" means we feel as if we are in a perpetual rut like Pig-Pen, who perpetually kept a cloud of dust around him; he was always dirty – pretty sure we could count on him having a dirty tush. But I admire Pig-Pen, and here's why: rather than sulking in misery – as we often do – about his inability to remain clean, he remained cheerful, and occasionally took steps to tidy his appearance and shake his cartoonish dust cloud.

The truth is sometimes we settle for unfriendly, however, controllable circumstances followed by our irritation for not being perfect. Disregard the insatiable pursuit of perfection. Do you want to know what that looks like? Simply put, it's you on a hamster wheel. And if you need another example, we still don't know how many licks it takes to get to the center of a Tootsie Pop. But, the moral of my story is that if you have "mud butt," you must take actions and steps to change your circumstances and clean your butt; it's okay to acknowledge the negative, but you must move on. Pig-Pen acknowledged his "mud butt," worked at it, but ultimately gained a greater appreciation of his life.

Change is a common denominator

throughout this book. Only, it's too bad 3/2 of people have trouble with fractions. The sheer beauty of life is that it is dynamic. You must overcome the addiction of apathy and complacency. Once you change your paradigm and re-channel your energy, the kaleidoscope changes like a shot of fresh air after a courtesy flush. For example, if you want to lose weight, then start by going for a walk. If you hate public speaking, then take a course in public speaking. If you don't know much about sports and want to share conversations with friends, or a cute guy or gal, then start watching ESPN's Sports Center. The genuine success you'll feel from personal accomplishment will be far,

far better than any red or blue pill the matrix can offer. Perhaps this sounds intuitive; however, how many of you are repeating the same actions, jobs, and habits but expecting and praying for a different outcome? That's the definition of insanity people. Yes, really. I'm just saying...

Flush

(2)

Women are better flushers (because they never doo-doo)

RESTROOMS

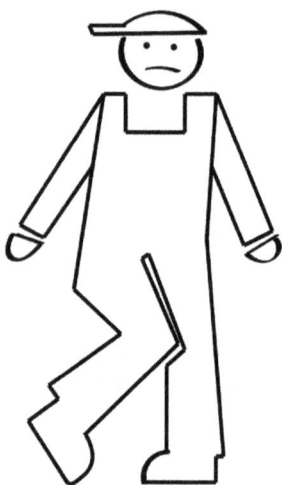

MEN   **WOMEN**

I've been with my wife for ten years now. I know, I know, quite the accomplishment. During that time we've had some amazing travels and experiences. But I've never seen my wife take a sweet deuce! As men we often comment about this fact: Do women ever drop deuces? See, it's not that women don't "go." Women have an uncanny wizardry of internal empathy – so much so – that they do everything in their power to prevent those around them from having to fall victim to their own stank-stank; it's actually quite beautiful.

For that reason, in this flush, I'm stressing the importance of keeping women around you – be it your job, your social life, your personal life, etc. I had a boss once who perceived women as overly emotional, and would characterize this as a negative trait. WRONG! On the contrary, this is what makes women great, especially if we find ourselves in a field or environment that requires soft-skills and emotional intelligence.

At times, men can be very sterile when assessing human activity and interactions. Why? From birth men are told not to cry and be "a big boy." Alternatively, women are consoled and learn it's okay to let emotions show. Women benefit like this: in some situations you can watch a woman figuratively take a "step back," take a panoramic view of a stressful situation, and dissect the situation with a calm, surgical precision. When you see this happen, you know it; and it is impressive to watch. Keeping women in your circle will give insight via osmosis to their hyper-awareness and hyper-empathy, which is vital to a more peaceful existence. Here's a fun bit of information to hit my point home: statistics constantly show that countries with more women in leadership positions are more peaceful countries. That's not an accidental flush. Cue the white doves.

Flush

(3)

White teeth
good, poo-poo
bad; Smiling
does wonders

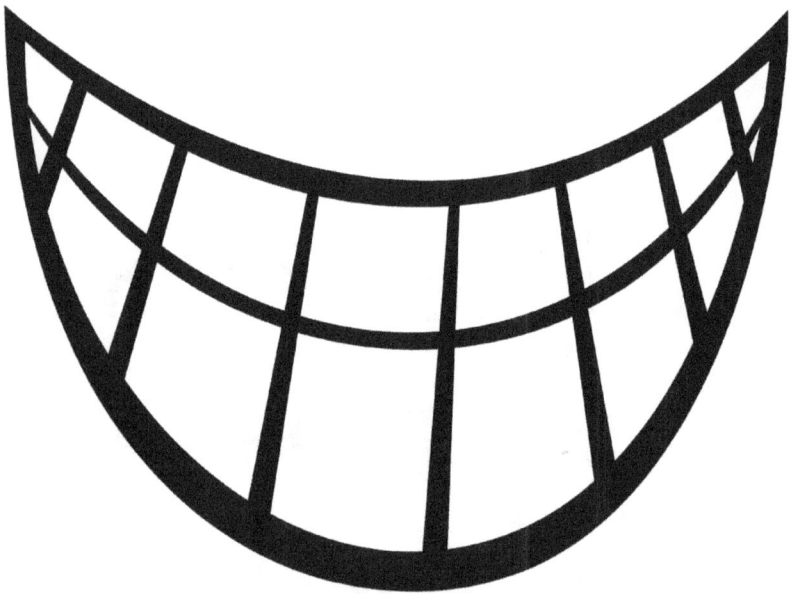

So I'm a nerd, right? I watch TV shows like National Geographic's Brain Games. During a segment of the show, the host took a small sample of people from a local mall to conduct a study. The study had the subjects examine a series of photos between two political candidates running for the same elected position. Of the two photos, the subjects had to guess solely from the pictures alone which candidate they believe ultimately won the political race/campaign. Note, the whole time the host knew the results of each election in the study. Why am I telling you this? Because what the host concluded, and the test subjects ultimately validated with their choices, is that the political candidates with bigger, better and brighter smiles tended to win those respective races more often than not.

I was shocked at how the test subjects –again – with no knowledge of the actual winner of those races, continued to pick winners simply off of headshots! If you haven't figured it out yet, the segment illustrated the importance of a smiling face, and the effect it has on human emotion and connection. Subconsciously, looking at people's smiles evokes empathy and a sense of connection. And, typically, the more white teeth we show results in a deeper emotional connection. In the future, try to be more conscious of your "bitchy resting face." And guys we have to watch that "mean mug" face. That's the "pooh-pooh" we need to flush.

Instead, smile and watch the astounding results. People will be nicer to you; your social interactions will increase and become more positive; people will give you free stuff. I'm super-serious about that last one, too. I get free stuff from people all the time just because of a simple smile. And people recognize that my smile is genuine. It's muy importante that your smile reflects genuine emotion. I'm not telling you to smile for the sake of being phony, but folks enjoy a smiling face as opposed to negativity, often seen on the first ten minutes of the local or world news (depressing much). Please smile often with, and at, people and then watch how much more you enjoy life – real talk.

Flush

④

Deal ...
Some people will
never courtesy
flush

Your mind can fool you into believing that all people generally act the same. Then you make generalizations and say things like nobody likes me, or these people are weird. This is the farthest from the truth. Your assumptions affect your stress-o-sphere and mood-station. It takes practice, but you have to pay close attention to people – people watch. For example, have you ever noticed some people are complete contrarians? I once had a colleague that fit that profile. On a clear day outside I said, "Hey, the sky sure is blue today." That colleague turned to me and said, "Aw, well, it's not really blue, but more like a periwinkle." You've also experienced the "Debby Downers" and "Negative

Nancys." These people perpetually are the bearers of bad news and negativity. They wallow in the smell. You could explain to them what a courtesy flush was, and the concept would pass them like a Blue Angels fly-over.

You've had these types of people around you for years and were unable to put a finger on what it was these individuals did to irritate you. Now you can start by making your life more peaceful. Pause. Observe. Deal. Manage these people. You will now mentally courtesy flush for them. Some people are just "odor blind." Realize there will be people in your life that you don't like, some people will always disagree with you, and others are naturally downers. That's their road. Stay in your lane. Because if you allow them to dictate how you feel by riding shotgun with them, it only leads to unhappiness, heartburn and a spiritual dead-end. Some people will never courtesy flush. And that's okay. Don't let it give you internal oppression. Like Taylor Swift says, just "shake it off."

Flush

⑤

Pre-flush: Compassion & Emotional Intelligence

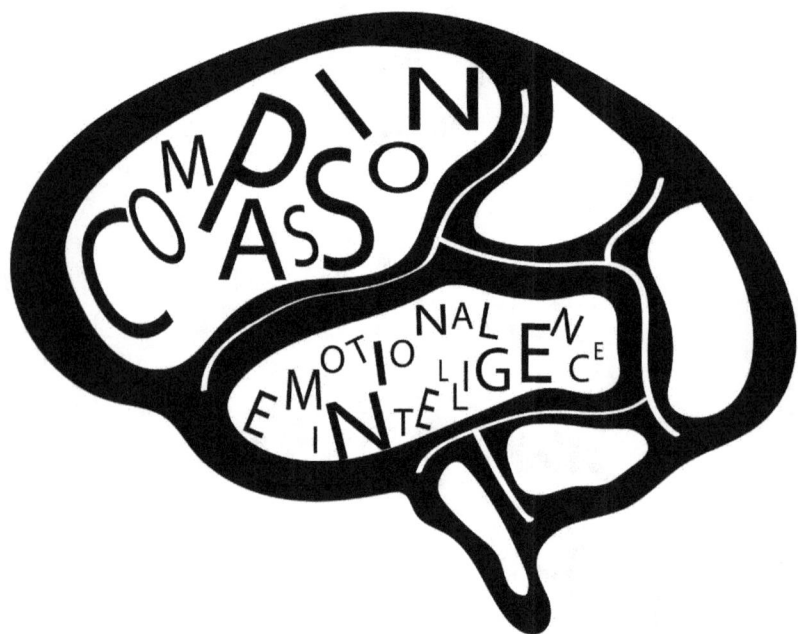

I hate to set one flush apart from the others because the sum is always greater than the part; however, if I created a Venn diagram, Flush #5 would definitely always be in the overlap. I'm often reminded of the beauty of "pre-flushes." I was in an audience that was instructed to close our eyes as the speaker told a tale of an individual afflicted by prejudice, discrimination and unequal opportunity. Near the end of his story, and right before he asked us to open our eyes, he said, "Now, picture that person is the same race and gender as you." As my eyes opened, I took a panoramic view of the room and noticed that some appeared to have tears welling up in their eyes;

others looked sad and confused. What that speaker did was give us a Class A, shock and awe, powerful example of compassion – internalizing and having sympathy for others sufferings and misfortunes. The speaker used race and gender because those are strong identifiers. But why do we sometimes need those identifiers for it to matter so deeply? Because it shouldn't!

For you to notice other people's misfortunes you have to work at this; it's not a "God-given talent." In a "microwave world" we never take the time to really ponder how others may feel. What are they going through? Why are they down or frustrated? Usually it's because we really don't care. Not being considerate and not having compassion for others reeks of diarrhea and "mud butt." Courtesy flush. Clean up. Show more compassion and watch the world open-up. From there, you will love, embrace and appreciate the human that is all of us, which will accentuate the positive in your life.

Pre-flushing also involves accentuating emotional intelligence. If emotional intelligence is a seed, then compassion is the water or the sun – essentially a part of the photosynthesis process. Emotional intelligence means that you take a concerted cognitive approach to managing your emotions, expressing yourself, and doing such in a manner that displays empathy when socializing or as part of the relationship building process. In the 9/11 aftermath, the world displayed a beautiful sense of compassion and emotional intelligence. The memories leave me nostalgic and intoxicated. As a world, we cried together, we held hands at national events, and we started real discussions, talking with one another as opposed to talking down or at each other.   Race didn't matter. Religion didn't matter. You saw emotional intelligence at its brightest. You saw what a world of courtesy flushes could look like. As you think quietly, please remember that the pre-flush is the compassion and emotional intelligence, which is just as important as the chicken or the egg.

Flush

(6)

Latto & Dino
have it right:
Poop and let it
go

Latto

Dino

Latto and Dino are my two French Bulldogs; they have great personalities. After Latto and Dino poop, both dogs want absolutely nothing to do with their waste, especially Latto. Both are notorious for pooping and darting-off stage left like they're trying to outrun the black plague – quickest courtesy flush ever. I don't blame them; I pick it up and it's wicked. No matter, my dogs act as my service-dogs. My wife and I welcomed Latto and Dino to our family after I was diagnosed with post-traumatic stress disorder (PTSD). I struggle at times, but my dogs are a major help. I've learned a lot from my doggies. Latto and Dino understand that poop rolls downhill. Watching their vanishing act after taking a deuce constantly reminds me that the bad, anxiety and worry should be dealt-with and done-with relatively quickly to prevent constipation.

You've been there. Have you ever let things build up so much that it affects your happiness and health? Don't let the paralysis by analysis build up. The build-up is unnecessary pressure and stress. The next thing you know, you're consumed by the multiplier effect of it all. If you're high diving into a pool don't worry about the height. Don't worry about the lifeguard's ability. Don't worry about the entrance into the water. Your primary concern should be can I swim? That's it! If you are confident in your swimming ability, don't waste time with the "don't matter stuff." Tell yourself to courtesy flush. Poop and let it go. Then watch your peace-of-mind build up. You see how the reciprocal works? Cool, right?

Flush

⑦

The Golden Rule: Nice always smells better

During the holiday season clandestine Santa Clauses all across the nation hand out free money, pay off layaway balances at stores for unsuspecting customers, and pass along big tips to members of the service industry. Nothing gives me a warmer feeling than the actions of these citizens. At my barbershop, I sometimes pay for other patrons, and I'll tell my barber to keep it a secret. Nice always smells better because it is an effective way to practice connecting with people. The action of being nice allows both giver and receiver to bask in the joy. It sounds idealistic but the "golden rule" – do onto others, as you would have them do onto you – is still a very effective compass towards the humanitarian North Star.

How do you feel when someone does something nice for you? How do you feel when you do something nice for another? Good on both ends, right? Robert Frost said, "The afternoon knows what the morning never suspected." You may not expect it, but nice actions often breed a chain reaction of nice actions from others; it becomes a picture that other people can trace. It becomes a picture of happiness. You'll notice that if you practice this at work, it becomes contagious, and then you have work-place excellence, for which you will be directly responsible. Try it. Practice it. You'll see art in motion.

Even better, nice is free. You can be nice with the intangibles. You can simply say thank you, open or hold the door for someone, pick up trash on the sidewalk, lift a heavy box for a struggling senior, or volunteer. Quite often you will find the things that cost nothing are often the most priceless. That definitely smells fresh.

Flush

(8)

Sometimes you have to flush twice as hard

You're probably thinking twice the work? Really? Or you're thinking – thanks, Ron – because I didn't need another homework assignment. But, actually, the opposite is true. What's nice takes twice. Yes, we sometimes have to put more of an effort into certain activities than others. For example, I can shoot a free throw with my eyes closed, but if you had asked me how to pronounce "quinoa" or explain women's fashion, I would look at you like you just asked me a $64,000 question. The title of Flush #8 suggests that if we rely on muscle memory and diligence, we can satisfy our inner peace, our inner confidence and build character.

You and I both have experienced hard times...boy have we ever! Even with emotional intelligence, white teeth and thinking about Latto and Dino, it still becomes hard to courtesy flush for yourself, let alone others. We get down. We lose our emotional equilibrium. We hope the toilet has motion detection, or is on automatic so that the decision and effort is taken out of our hands.

This is where muscle memory contributes to character. Character describes who we are in times of adversity, not who we are when things are peachy and a white-mocha latte. Therefore, let muscle memory and diligence act as your Rock of Gibraltar. In other words, flushing twice as hard is the foundation on which character is built. The process doesn't have to be the punishment. If anger is the enemy of your progress, then count to ten during periods of "mud butt." Do breathing exercises. Meditation. Or take up yoga. Again, the prescription is practice and persistence. The more persistent you are with these types of activities, you'll notice areas of your life start to flow more easily. You will be more patient, peaceful and confident. Decisions will cause you less angst. For example, Gandhi and Martin Luther King, Jr. had to practice non-violence, establishing bitter roots but the fruit was sweet. Gandhi said it best, "First they ignore you, then they laugh at you, then they fight you, then you win." Let me put his words in another context. Don't ignore your frustrations. Work at them. Don't laugh it off or listen to others. Push forward. Don't fight progress. Don't fight yourself. You will always lose. Win now. Champions are made on the practice field and when the cameras are off. When you're in that stall, it's only you, and nobody else. Will you take the easy wrong, or the hard right? Think twice.

Flush

⑨

It's okay to call
the plumber:
The hard part
of generosity is
receiving it

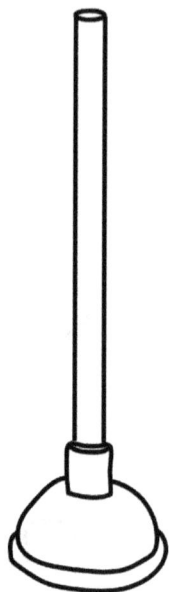

Every day 22 U.S. military veterans commit suicide. That's one veteran every 65 minutes. Even as I write this now, the thought is extremely hard for me and evokes emotion. Veterans – including myself with PTSD – can be very independent people; we quite often refrain from asking others for help. That is our greatest strength and our greatest weakness. One theory says the real issue is that we don't get help until we hit rock bottom, if we even get help at all.

To be clear – I'm not comparing war with receiving a parking ticket or a tough break-up. The point here is no matter what your circumstances are there are individuals and resources available. The first step is that you must learn to trust and trust others to help. You must engage though. Become a participator of your life as opposed to a viewer. The hardest part of generosity is receiving it, but by giving into receiving help, you get more. It's so true. I tried to deal with my personal afflictions for years by myself. It wasn't working. I was burning up my mental hard drive. I gained weight. My stress went from zero to one hundred in sixty seconds. My next move was my best move. I called a plumber. In my situation, the plumber was a counselor and now my flush system works much more efficiently. I can courtesy flush and not worry that my system will tank.

There are so many professionals in the world that are amazing at providing us with the resources and help we desperately need. For example, there are life-coaches, doctors, therapists, nutritionists, authors, etc. You may not receive instant gratification but, as a Chinese proverb says, "Good things take time." In other words, you need to put the microwave away and start using your oven, which makes the food taste better if you ask me. Yes, the oven takes longer, I know. But, as an analogy to your life, you'll notice beauty in the journey. By taking footstep by footstep, the air becomes more breathable like that first breath of fresh air after a dust storm. I learned a lesson a long time ago with respect to plumbing and home renovations: when you try to fix something yourself and it doesn't work, you pay the plumber twice as much – once for the actual fix and another for repairing your "fix."

Flush

(10)

Courtesy Flush

PLEASE
COURTESY
FLUSH

Bust out the streamers and balloons, preferably while you're on the toilet seat. Nothing left to do now but pull the lever.   Over the course of this book you've learned to show those pearly whites more often; appreciate the female species great sixth sense; not settle for where you are, but where you want to be; deal with and manage those who cause us to flush; be nice because the benefits trickle up and down; flush harder for things worth flushing for; appreciate Latto and Dino's perspective; demonstrate compassion and emotional intelligence for all; and appreciate gratitude and help.

Yet, my words are only the picture.

Hopefully it's not too difficult to trace. Don't worry how you labeled yourself in the past. I hate labels. Labels have consequences because labels put us in a box. The box is a funny mirror house, and you constantly see yourself as distorted. Forget that! Get moving now! Big things have small beginnings. My wish is for you to find true happiness. Use the tools I've provided because the return-on-investment can be awesome! I'm talking peace. I'm talking health. I'm talking contentment. I'm talking liberation. I'm talking you! I speak from the heart. So, please, take my heart-felt strategies. One love. One flush.

Fair winds
and following
seas

What is your

courtesy

flush level?

Check off every statement you agree with. When you are finished, count how many of each symbol you checked to determine your flush level.

- ☐ ○ I see the glass half-empty
- ☐ □ I see the glass half-full
- ☐ ◊ I never hold doors
- ☐ △ I say "thank you" and "I appreciate you" to the service industry
- ☐ ○ I let cars merge from time-to-time
- ☐ △ I give up my seat on a bus or train for the elderly or disabled
- ☐ □ I say "good morning," "good afternoon" or "good evening"
- ☐ ◊ I blow my car horn as the traffic light switches to green
- ☐ △ I volunteer
- ☐ □ I donate
- ☐ □ I mentor
- ☐ ◊ It is easier to give up on tasks
- ☐ ◊ A little gossip is good
- ☐ □ I share information others may find valuable
- ☐ ○ I think some people are just too nice
- ☐ ○ I don't care what others think of me
- ☐ ◊ Most people aren't as smart as me
- ☐ ◊ I find it weird to smile at people as they pass me
- ☐ ◊ We don't know nice where I'm from
- ☐ ○ Chicks dig bad boys
- ☐ ○ Money makes me happy
- ☐ △ I think quality over quantity
- ☐ ○ Being kind is way too much work
- ☐ ◊ It's okay if my kids bump into you and don't say

excuse me

- [ ] ◊ I don't feel any emotion while watching the first 10 minutes of the news
- [ ] ○ Fool me once, shame on you. Fool me twice, shame on me.
- [ ] ○ Tranquility doesn't exist
- [ ] ○ Life is meant to be tough
- [ ] ◊ When I'm walking people should move out of my way
- [ ] ◊ I think women are too emotional
- [ ] □ I've paid for a stranger's meal
- [ ] □ I've offered leftovers to homeless
- [ ] Δ I tell someone I love them every day
- [ ] ◊ I check my phone while having a face-to-face conversation with someone
- [ ] Δ I see kindness as a universal language

1 flush   x   (# of ◊) _____   =   _____
2 flushes x   (# of ○) _____   =   _____
3 flushes x   (# of □) _____   =   _____
4 flushes x   (# of Δ) _____   =   _____

TOTAL SUM = _____

0-10 flushes: You need heavy toilet paper, a plunger, air freshener, and a double flush. What did you eat?

10-25 flushes: You've got a decent turd mountain, but keep flushing accordingly. Caution! You can still cause trouble in a small bathroom!

25+ flushes: Your stall must be empty, because there's no smell coming from you! No fan necessary!

"I'd rather be a young fool than an old fool."

"Hesitation will only get you

nowhere."

"Don't let the bridges you cross be the bridges you burn."

"You do not become a hero overnight, but just a step at a time."

"Life is sweat equity: you get what you put in."

"Just because you feel worthless doesn't mean you can't end up meaningful."

"Success = hard work. There are no coincidences — only the illusion of coincidence."

Suggested Readings

THE FOLLOWING ARE A FEW OF MY FAVORITE RELATED BOOKS THAT CAN HELP ON THE FLUSH STRATEGIES MENTIONED IN THIS BOOK.

Bailey, Joseph. *The Serenity Principle*. San Francisco: Harper & Row, 1990

Barra, Allen. *The Last Coach*. New York: Norton Paperback, 2006

Carlson, Richard. *Don't Sweat the Small Stuff...and it's all small stuff*. New York: MJF Books, 1997

Carlson, Richard. *You Can Be Happy No Matter What*. San Rafael, Calif.: New World Library, 1992

Chopra, Deepak. *The Seven Spiritual Laws of Success*. San Rafael, Calif.: New World Library, 1994

Dungy, Tony. *The Mentor Leader*. Carol Stream, IL: Tyndale House Publishers, Inc., 2010

About the Author

Ron Holloway is a Navy Veteran and public speaker best known for his short books that are part of the newest literary trend, which make those with short attention spans very happy. Ron grew up in Milwaukee, Wisconsin, traveled all over the world, and now resides in the Washington, D.C. metropolitan area with his wife and their two French bulldogs.

Stay Updated

iamronholloway.com

Two non-profit organizations will receive a portion of all book proceeds for the life of the book: Operation Smile and Hero Dogs.

www.ingramcontent.com/pod-product-compliance
Lightning Source LLC
Chambersburg PA
CBHW070643030426
42337CB00020B/4140